Martina

Rupert and Werner

Maria, Pussy and Agathe

Johanna with Bella
(2 months old)

Werner with Bella
(6 months old)

Martina with bella
(One year old)

For Maria A. von Trapp
and her unforgettable family

Hans Wilhelm

The Trapp Family Book

HEINEMANN : LONDON

William Heinemann Ltd
10 Upper Grosvenor Street, London W1X 9PA
LONDON   MELBOURNE   TORONTO
JOHANNESBURG   AUCKLAND

First published in Great Britain 1983
Text and illustrations © by Hans Wilhelm Inc. 1983
434 97248 7

Reprinted 1985

Phototypeset by Tradespools Ltd, Frome, Somerset
Printed in Hong Kong by
Wing King Tong Co. Ltd

Viva La Musica!

Michael Praetorius

Three parts

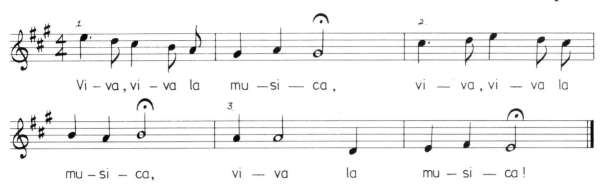

Vi – va, vi – va la   mu –si – ca,   vi — va , vi — va la

mu –si – ca,   vi — va   la   mu — si — ca!

My any years ago, in the convent of Nonnberg in the beautiful old town of Salzburg in Austria, a young girl called Maria was preparing to become a nun.

Maria was deeply religious; but she was also full of fun, and loved singing and playing the guitar. She was eager to learn and did her best to do what she was told, but it wasn't always easy for her to obey the strict rules of the convent. Sometimes she was late for early morning mass – and once or twice she missed it altogether. She would wake up feeling that she just had to get out into the sunshine. Then she would slip out from behind the dark high walls of the convent and climb up into the mountains to watch the sunrise and sing to her guitar. Mass was quite forgotten – though when the Reverend Mother spoke to her afterwards she was always repentant.

One day the Reverend Mother called Maria to her room. Maria thought she was going to be scolded again for being late for mass.

But the Reverend Mother had a surprise for her. "Maria, my child," she said, "I have decided to send you away for a while. I have had a letter from Baron von Trapp who lives not far from here. He was a captain in the navy, and sadly is a widower with seven children. One of his little daughters is not very strong, and he can't find anyone to look after her. He has asked me if I could spare someone from the convent to help him for a while. I would like you to go." Seeing Maria's crestfallen face, she went on, "Don't be unhappy. It's only for a short time, and you won't be far away. You'll be back here next summer."

Maria didn't want to leave the convent, for it had become her home, but she knew she must obey the Reverend Mother. Tearfully, she changed her clothes and packed her precious guitar with her few belongings.

The heavy wooden doors of the convent closed behind her. She climbed down the steps from the convent to Salzburg where she took a bus to Aigen.

By late afternoon she had reached the great gates of the Captain's estate. Peering through the iron bars at the wide lawns, Maria saw the lines of tall dark trees, and the grand house at the end of the drive.

She walked up to the front door feeling very uneasy. Her hand trembled as she rang the doorbell.

She was shown in by a servant. There before her in the hall stood the Captain. He welcomed her with a kind smile, but Maria was too nervous to say a word. She was most alarmed when the Captain drew a whistle out of his pocket and blew it. Whatever could he be doing? But that was only the Captain's way of summoning his children. They came running down the stairs, all seven of them, and the Captain introduced them in order, from the tallest down. "Rupert, Agathe, Maria, Werner, Hedwig, Johanna and Martina." Each child bowed in greeting as the Captain called its name.

"I'm afraid they aren't usually so well behaved," said the Captain with a sigh. "They get up to such tricks – white mice, frogs, wet sponges, ghosts . . . I just hope you won't be frightened away like the twenty-five young ladies who were here before you."

Maria was *very* frightened, but she managed a small smile.

"Now the children will show you to your room," said the Captain, and Maria slowly followed them up the stairs.

That night Maria hardly slept a wink. She tossed and turned as the Captain's words went round and round in her head. What kind of

tricks were the children planning to play on her? It was four years since their mother had died and they had had twenty-five nurses and governesses! The last one had stayed only two months! When at last Maria did doze off, it was to dream of frogs and white mice . . .

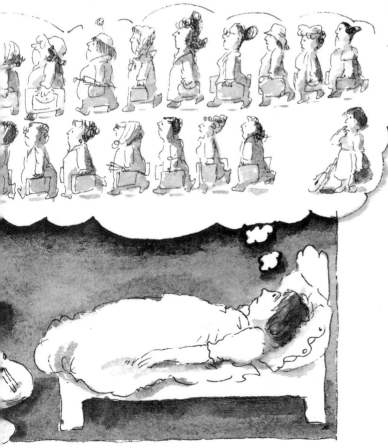

Morning Is Come

English folk song

Four Parts

Morn-ing is come, night is a — way,

Rise with the sun — and wel - come the day.

When Maria woke up the next morning, the dark rain clouds had disappeared and sunlight was streaming into her room. Her bad dreams forgotten, she jumped out of bed to open the window and let in the fresh mountain air. She felt so good that she reached out for her guitar, plucked softly at the strings, and began to sing.

As the sound of Maria's sweet voice filled the house, Captain von Trapp's children stopped what they were doing. They had never heard such music. They tiptoed to Maria's door and looked in. Maria took no notice but went on singing as the children stood there and listened, entranced. The servants gathered behind them. Even the Captain came to listen. And still Maria sang.

"Please, sister Maria, will you teach us to sing like that?" said Hedwig when at last Maria put down her guitar.

"Yes, sister Maria, I would like the children to learn to sing," said the Captain.

"If you really mean it, we could start today after school," said Maria shyly.

That first day was exhausting. Maria was expected to give lessons to the two youngest children, Martina – who was very delicate – and Johanna. She had to make sure that the older children were neatly dressed and got to school on time. When they came home, she had to supervise them and see that they did their homework.

Maria was afraid they would not do what she told them, and that the Captain would be angry.

She need not have worried. The children raced through their homework so that the singing lesson could begin. The next day they wanted another lesson. Maria found that they all had sweet voices and could hold a tune. From then on, nothing could stop the von Trapp children singing.

They practised their scales as Maria taught them, and learned the words of all the songs she knew. They began to learn songs with several parts, so that they could sing in harmony.

They were so busy practising that they had no time to be naughty. Anyway, they liked Maria too much to play tricks on her.

As for Maria, she was busy too – so busy that she had no time to be homesick for the convent. She soon felt quite at home with the von Trapp family, even with the Captain. As summer slipped into autumn and then winter, she came to cherish evenings round the fire, when she would tell stories to the children and the Captain would sit in his big armchair, smoking a pipe and listening and watching. He had been unable to spend much time with the children since their mother died, but now that Maria was here he tried to be with them whenever possible. She realized that he was glad of her presence, and that despite his formal manner, and his startling habit of blowing a whistle to summon his children, he was a kind and gentle man.

Maria had always loved Christmas, and she was determined that this one should be the best the children had ever had. They were eager to learn Christmas carols to sing to the household, and Maria soon had them busy practising. She knew how to make all kinds of exciting things – such as a big Advent wreath. She showed them how to twine fir branches into a wreath and decorate it with ribbons and four candles, one to be lit on each of the four Sundays before Christmas.

Outside, the cold grew fierce, and the winter wind whistled down the chimneys. Icicles hung from the roof and window-ledges. The children went out to play in the snow, muffled in heavy coats and scarves, and made an enormous snowman.

Inside, the great house hummed with activity. There hadn't been such whispering, so many secrets, or such happy laughter for a long time. With Maria's help, the children threw themselves into making presents and decorations for Christmas. There was hammering and sawing and gluing, painting, sewing and writing going on behind closed doors all over the house all day long. In the evenings the children would gather together to practise carols.

Down in the kitchen the cook was busy making Christmas cakes, gingerbread men, and all kinds of sweets and biscuits. When the children came in from school they were greeted by delicious smells, and rushed downstairs to help or to taste something as it came out of the oven. The kitchen was the best place to be, and it was always full of people – the cook, the maids, the gardener, Maria, and sometimes even the Captain.

Maria suggested the children made *Lebkuchen* themselves. *Lebkuchen* are traditional cakes that are always made at Christmas in Austria. This is how they are made:

First dissolve 15 gm. (½ oz) of bicarbonate of soda in a little rose water or milk. Then mix together in a large bowl 750 gm. (1½ lbs) of flour with a teaspoon of cinnamon, and one and a half teaspoons of ground cloves and a pinch of cardamom. Meanwhile, someone else should stir together four eggs and 500 gm. (1 lb) of sugar in another large bowl until light and foamy. Now add to the eggs and sugar mixture 250 gm. (½ lb) of honey, 100 gm. (4 oz) candied peel and 375 gm. (12 oz) of ground almonds and the dissolved bicarbonate of soda and stir well. Then finally mix in the flour with a pinch of salt. Mix together well and knead into a smooth dough.

Roll out the dough on a floured board to the thickness of your little finger (you may not have room to do it all at once) and cut it into squares or little Christmas shapes. Lay them on a greased baking tray and stand in a cool place overnight. The next day bake them in the oven at a medium heat for about 25 minutes.

When cool, you can decorate the *Lebkuchen* with almonds and icing.

Oh Christmas Tree
Traditional German carol

Oh   Christmas tree, Oh Christmas tree, With faithful leaves un — chang-ing ;   Not

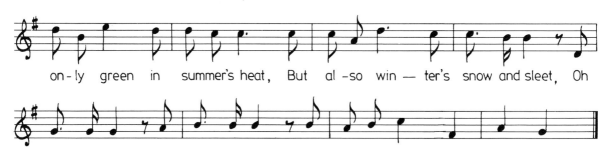

on-ly   green   in   summer's heat, But   al -so win — ter's   snow and sleet,   Oh

Christmas tree ,   Oh   Christmas tree ,   With   faithful leaves   un — chang-ing .

2. Oh Christmas tree, oh Christmas tree,
Of all the trees most lovely;
Each year, you bring to me delight
Shining bright on Christmas night.
Oh Christmas tree, oh Christmas tree,
Of all the trees most lovely.

3. Oh Christmas tree, oh Christmas tree,
Your leaves will teach me, also,
That hope and love and faithfulness
Are precious things I can possess.
Oh Christmas tree, oh Christmas tree,
Your leaves will teach me also.

A few days before Christmas Eve, Maria asked the Captain to bring home a Christmas tree – one of the tall fir trees that bordered his estate. The Captain took his axe and trudged through the snow till he found the tallest and straightest tree. Then he chopped it down and dragged it back to the house.

The night before Christmas Eve, when the seven children had gone to sleep, Maria set to work to decorate the tree, hanging it with shimmering baubles and silvery tinsel. She put candles, golden nuts, small apples, *Lebkuchen* and pieces of marzipan on all the branches, and placed a great golden star at the very top.

The next morning Maria and the family went early to church, walking through the crisp snow to the village. The children were not allowed in to see the tree until the evening.

When the doors opened, they saw the beautiful tree in the candlelight. Then the children had all the fun of unwrapping their presents and discovering what the others had made for them. Afterwards Maria and the children gave a concert of carols.

Silent Night

Austrian carol

Si — lent night, Ho — ly night, All is calm, all is bright;

'Round yon vir — gin mo-ther and child, Ho — ly In -fant so ten -der and mild,

Sleep in heavenly peace,_____ Sleep in heavenly peace.

2. Silent night, Holy night,
Shepherds quake at the sight;
Glories stream from heaven afar,
Heav'nly hosts sing Alleluia!
Christ the Saviour is born!
Christ the Saviour is born!

3. Silent night, Holy night,
Son of God, love's pure light;
Radiance beams from Thy holy face,
With the dawn of redeeming grace,
Jesus, Lord at Thy birth,
Jesus, Lord, at Thy birth.

Late in the evening the Captain lit a lantern for each of the children and they walked through the snow to the church for Midnight Mass. This time Maria was not with them. She had gone to Nonnberg to celebrate mass with the sisters.

Just as she had hoped, it had been the best Christmas the von Trapp children had ever had.

The Lark in the Morn

English folk song

As I was a — walk — ing one morning in the spring, I met a pret-ty dam — sel, so sweetly she did sing; And as we were a — walk -ing un – to me this did she say, "There is no life like the plough — boy's all in the month of May."

So the winter months passed, and at last the snow melted and it was spring again. Maria took the children for long walks in the mountains. They wandered in fields bright with flowers and butterflies, and the sound of their clear voices rang in the fresh mountain air as Maria led the singing.

The von Trapp children were singing better than ever. Music was a joy to all of them, and Maria felt grateful that through singing the family had accepted her.

These were happy days, but for Maria there was a shadow over them. She knew there was only a little time left before she must return to Nonnberg. The Reverend Mother had promised her that she would be back in the convent before summer.

That was what Maria had wanted – but things had changed. She told herself that she still wanted to be a nun, but she could hardly bear to think of leaving the von Trapp children. They were as dear to her as her own family.

When she broke the news of her departure, the children were heartbroken. They could not believe that their beloved Maria would abandon them.

Maria tried to forget her sadness as she helped the servants with the spring-cleaning. While she was working, the three youngest children came up to her and said something, but she was so busy she didn't listen properly. She answered, "Yes. Yes," and they ran away.

The next moment the Captain stood beside her, beaming, delighted she had accepted his proposal of marriage. Maria was so shocked she dropped her duster and stared at him in disbelief.

The children had decided that the only way they could keep Maria for ever would be if she and their father married. They had asked him about this and he had replied that he would like to

marry Maria but he didn't know whether she liked him. So they had asked Maria and returned to their father to shout triumphantly that she did!

However, Maria had truly grown to love the Captain too and, after she had received the blessing of the Reverend Mother, she accepted his proposal.

Maria and Georg von Trapp were married on an autumn day. The wedding took place at Nonnberg, where Maria had spent such happy years. The sisters helped her dress in her wedding gown and came to the church to join in the marriage service. The seven children were there, and Johanna and Martina carried

Maria's train. The Captain was
dressed in full uniform.

The bells rang out, the organ
played, and all Salzburg rejoiced
with the newly-wed couple.

The Echo Yodel
Austrian folk song

He - i - ti, (Ho - i - ti), halt's Mäu, sei schtü, i geh hoam, wann i wü.

He - i - ti, (Ho - i - ti), halt's Mäu, sei schtü, i geh hoam, wann i wü.

He - i - ti, (Ho - i - ti), halt's Mäu, sei schtü, i geh hoam, wann i wü.

He - i - ti, (Ho - i - ti), halt's Mäu, sei schtad, sei schtü.

"And so they were married, and lived happily ever after." That is the way that fairy tales end. But the story of the von Trapps really only begins with the wedding. The wedding made them a real family – a family that sang together.

In the old days, the Captain used to spend his days alone in the great house, while the children went off on their own. But now he had discovered, through Maria, how much fun it was to be with his family. He enjoyed going for walks and picnics and bicycle rides with them. And now, when they sang, he added his fine voice to the family choir. The family spent a wonderful summer together.

Another autumn and Christmas passed. Then there was another excitement for the children to look forward to – the birth of a new baby! Rosemarie was born in the spring, and two years later Maria gave birth to another girl, called Eleonore. Now there were two more voices to add to the family choir.

Those were happy years, but they were soon to end. Austria was facing a difficult time; the whole country was running out of cash. Many businesses collapsed and some of the banks closed down and went bankrupt, including the bank of the von Trapp family.

One dark day, the Captain realized that all his money was gone. He was desperately worried. However would he manage, with nine children to support and no income?

Maria comforted him. With her strong faith in God, she never doubted that they would be all right. She began to think of ways they could earn a living. As they still had the big house, she decided to take in lodgers. They could no longer afford servants to run it, but she worked hard herself and made sure that all the children did their share of cleaning it and looking after the lodgers. The Captain's strength and courage gradually returned to him and the family drew even closer together as they weathered the difficult years.

All of them found comfort in music, and valued more than ever the hours spent singing together. One day their songs were heard by someone who knew a great deal about music – a young priest called Father Wasner. He was very impressed by the pure sound they made.

Blue Monday
Austrian folk song

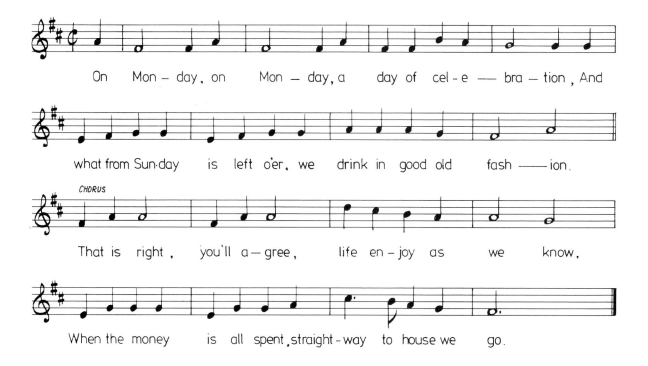

On Mon - day, on Mon - day, a day of cel - e — bra — tion, And

what from Sun-day is left o'er, we drink in good old fash ——— ion.

CHORUS

That is right, you'll a — gree, life en — joy as we know,

When the money is all spent, straight - way to house we go.

2. On Tuesday, on Tuesday, we then can sleep 'til nine,
   Then comes the master's daughter fair, snugs into bed of mine.
      That is right, you'll agree, etc.

3. On Wednesday, on Wednesday, the money is all gone,
   And when the master finds new work, Midweek again's begun.

4. On Thursday, on Thursday, the week begins in earnest,
   And when the meat is eaten up, the bones can taste the finest.

5. On Friday, on Friday, the mistress bakes the fish then,
   And even tho' we did not work, we join at dinner with them.

6. On Saturday, on Saturday, the week at last is ended,
   And when the bell strikes one o'clock, our hands are washed and cleaned.

7. On Sunday, on Sunday, the master's boasts are mounting,
   But when it comes to add our pay, he is not good at counting.

Father Wasner was able to give them some expert tuition, and under his guidance the family choir grew even better. But it never occurred to them to sing for an audience – until they got a new lodger.

The lodger was a world-famous singer who had come to take part in the annual music festival in Salzburg. When she heard the singing of the von Trapp family, she suggested that they should enter for the song contest at the festival. Captain von Trapp was horrified at the idea of his family appearing in public, but he talked it over with Maria, and finally agreed to let them take part.

There was hardly any time to rehearse, and none of them thought they stood a chance of winning a prize! However, it would be fun to meet other musicians and singers and make new friends.

Maria was determined that they should give the best performance they could, so she made the children spend every spare moment practising. They went over and over the traditional folk songs they were to sing at the contest until they were perfect.

The children had been looking forward to the concert, but when they saw the streets of Salzburg decorated with garlands and colourful banners for the festival, and realized that the concert hall was packed with people who would be listening to them singing, they were terrified. Maria did her best to calm them, but even she felt nervous as they sat and listened to the other competitors. The standard was so high that she wished they had never come.

"We don't belong in such company," she thought. "We should never have entered the contest."

The von Trapps came almost at the end of the programme, but at last their names were called and Maria led the family on to the stage.

With the bright lights shining down and hundreds of eyes looking at them, the family felt very alone in the middle of the big stage. They had such bad stage fright that afterwards none of them could remember anything about the performance. But they

sang the songs they had worked so hard on, and were aware of the applause as they stumbled off the stage. Their one desire was to go home. But first they had to return to their seats for the prizegiving.

Viva La Musica!

Michael Praetorius   Three parts

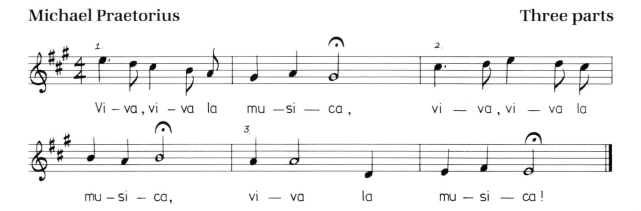

Vi – va, vi – va la mu – si – ca, vi — va, vi — va la

mu – si – ca, vi — va la mu – si – ca!

As the judges came on to the stage to announce the winner the audience fell silent.

"FIRST PRIZE FOR THE VON TRAPP FAMILY FROM SALZBURG!"

"It's not true," Maria gasped. "It must be a mistake." But it was no mistake. The family had to climb back on to the stage, to receive congratulations from the judges and tremendous applause from the audience.

It was a great day for all of them. Although the Captain was proud that his family had won first prize, he had not enjoyed the experience. He did not want them to sing again in public. None of them dreamed what the contest would lead to . . .

The contest had made the von Trapp family famous. They were invited to give a broadcast – and could not refuse.

By chance they were heard by the Austrian Chancellor, who liked the family choir so much that he asked them to sing for him at a reception in Vienna.

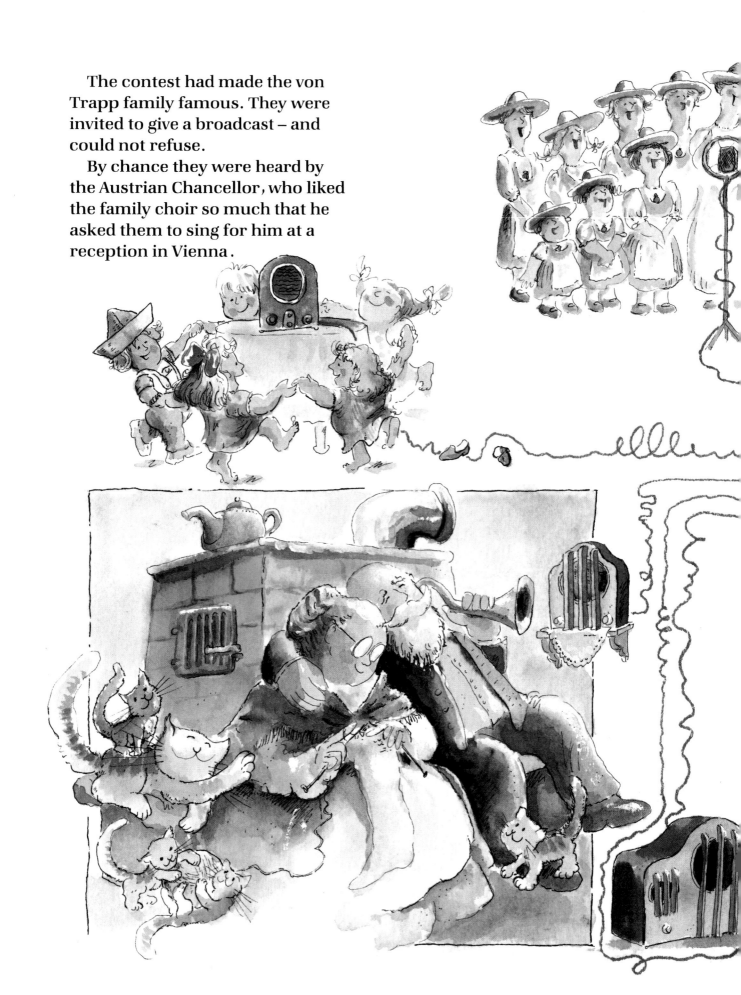

The von Trapps were pleased and honoured to receive this invitation, but their first instinct was to refuse. Stage fright had spoiled their first performance for them, and besides, they liked being at home. But they were finally persuaded to go to Vienna where they had a great success.

The following year they sang at the Salzburg Music Festival.

Their performances were praised by the critics and offers to perform came pouring in from all over Europe, and even one from America.

Captain von Trapp was still reluctant to travel and perform professionally. Also Maria feared that everything would change, and the family life they cherished so

much would be spoiled. But they
decided to make just one tour,
that would include Paris, London,
Brussels, The Hague, Milan, Turin,
Assisi and Rome. The tour was a
triumph, and the family had a
wonderful time. They had a warm
reception wherever they went,
made many new friends, and
enjoyed getting to know different
places.

Then, a few months later,
Austria was invaded by the
Germans.

52

Although many Austrians, hoping for a better future, cheered the marching troops, their dreams were soon crushed. The new rulers used Hitler's system of secret police to control the country with terror. No one knew any longer whom they could trust. Those who resisted the new laws put their lives and their families in danger.

The old Austrian anthem was banned and the beautiful voices of the von Trapp choir were silenced by the sound of heavy marching boots and the harsh tunes of martial music.

One morning Captain von Trapp received a letter from the German Navy department asking him to take over command of one of their new submarines.

But the Captain could not even think of accepting their offer after what they had done to his country.

Soon afterwards the family received an invitation to sing at Hitler's birthday party. To refuse was impossible.

That night they gathered in secret to talk about what they should do. They realized that there was only one way out. They must leave Austria. It was a terrible decision. They would have to say goodbye to all their friends, their beautiful home and all their possessions. They knew that if they managed to escape, they might never be able to return to their homeland. Yet they could not betray their country.

They remembered the invitation to give a tour in America. This

54

Innsbruck, ich muss dich lassen

Traditional Austrian song

Inns-bruck, ich muss dich las — sen, ich fahr da-hin mein Stra — ssen in frem-de Land da — hin. Mein Freud ist mir ge — nom — men, die ich nit weiss be — kom — men, wo ich im E - - - - - lend bin!

Gross Leid muss ich ertragen,
Das ich allein tu klagen
Dem liebsten Buhlen mein.
Ach Lieb, nun lass mich Armen
Im Herzen dein erbarmen,
Dass ich muss ferne sein!

Mein Trost ob allen Weiben,
Dein tu ich ewig bleiben,
Stet, treu, in Ehren fromm.
Nun müss dich Gott bewahren,
In aller Tugend sparen,
Bis dass ich wiederkomm!

would give them a place to go and enough to live on for a few months. After that, they must just have faith that their music would continue to support them.

They began to make plans for life in a new land, keeping their flight secret so that no one could try and stop them at the last moment. However, they confided in Father Wasner who decided to go with them and continue to help them with their music.

And so the von Trapp family left their home and their beloved country.

They told everyone that they were going on a walking holiday in the Alps, as they often did. This meant that, in order not to arouse

suspicion, they could carry only a little money and very few of their possessions.

They left the big house and set out over the mountains. They slipped across the frontier into Italy at a point where there were no guards.

Leaving Home
German folk song

Oh it's slow-ly I go through the thick fal-ling snow, Thick falling snow, Leaving

home and love be-hind. I must journey a-way thro' the dark winter's day,

Dark winter's day, With the snow and tears half blind. In this world we can't do

as we please, Or I would stay near you. But when fruit hangs golden and

ripe on the trees, Ripe on the trees, I will wed you if you're true.

2. As for me, I shall be ever faithful, you'll see,
Faithful you'll see,
Though other girls are fair;
They are many and kind, yet I'll never one find,
Never one find
Can with you, my dear, compare.
In this world we can't do as we please,
Or I would stay near you.
But when fruit hangs golden and ripe on the trees,
Ripe on the trees,
I will wed you if you're true.

The Captain had taken with him the precious letter inviting the von Trapp family to sing in America and as soon as they were settled in Italy he wrote asking for money to be sent for their fares across the Atlantic. He had to find a new home for Maria soon, for she was expecting another baby.

At last the letter they all longed for arrived, with money and tickets for the crossing, and the family set off on the next part of their journey. They had first to make their way to London where they were to board the liner *American Farmer*. As they thankfully settled themselves into their cabins, they felt safe for the first time for weeks.

The *American Farmer* was only a small ship, and the voyage took two weeks. It was rough at first and the children were seasick, but soon the weather cleared up and the von Trapps ventured up on deck and enjoyed the fresh sea breeze. It was like the first breath of freedom.

To help while away the time, the family tried to learn a little English from fellow passengers, but they found it difficult to pick up.

As they sailed into New York Harbour, the von Trapps were up on deck with the other passengers, gazing at the skyscrapers that towered above the waterfront, and the Statue of Liberty holding her torch of freedom high. As the ship sailed past, she seemed to be saying "Welcome" to the homeless family.

It was exciting to be there, but New York seemed huge and terrifying. Everything was so different: the crowds of people, the noise, the tall buildings. The von Trapps felt confused and homesick for their quiet mountains and valleys with the fresh clean air and lovely flowers.

Life in the New World was not easy for the von Trapps. They had very little money left, they could speak little English, and although they had made friends with several Americans on the boat, they had no close friends to whom they could turn for help. But there was no going back. Helped by their trust in God – and a thick dictionary – the von Trapp family slowly grew accustomed to life in America.

As soon as they had settled into their hotel, they began to rehearse. They worked day and night, knowing that their whole future depended on the success of their concerts in America.

One morning a big blue bus pulled up outside their hotel and the von Trapps climbed in, cramming in all their luggage and musical instruments as best they could. They were off on their first American tour.

Those first performances were not as successful as they had hoped. Their songs were too long and too serious for the audiences. The critics said nice things, but the theatres were half empty. But the von Trapps did not want to change their programme, nor did they want to wear other costumes or special stage make-up, as people suggested. Then the tour had to be cut short when the baby, Johannes, was born.

Maria and the Captain were worried about money. They had only been allowed into America for a short time and would have to leave soon. Where would they go and what would become of them?

Luckily, an offer came from Scandinavia and they set sail again across the Atlantic, back to Europe. It was the summer of 1939, just before the outbreak of World War II. That summer the von Trapps learned not to let their worries show in the way they sang.

One invitation led to another, and the von Trapps began to feel more confident that they could earn a living from giving concerts. The following spring they received another invitation to tour the United States. For the second time they set off for America – hoping that this time they would be allowed to stay there for good.

THE TRAPP FAMILY SINGERS

Welcome, Welcome!

American folk song

Four parts

1. Welcome, welcome ev'—ry guest, wel-come to our mu-sic fest,

2. Mu—sic is our plea-sant cheer, fills both soul and ra-vished ear.

3. Sa—cred Nine teach us thy mood, sweetest notes to be ex—plored.

4. Soft-ly fill the eve-ning air, to complete our con-cert fair!

The new tours went better. The von Trapps had learned not to be so serious when they sang. Their programme was brightened up with some popular folk songs. They realized that they needed to wear make-up in the strong glare of the stage lights.

They discovered that it wasn't enough to perform the songs well: they had to make the audience feel they were singing just for them.

The big blue bus travelled all round the country, full of children and luggage. Father Wasner was always with them and rehearsed new songs which enlarged their repertoire.

It felt good to be earning their living in a new country, especially as they were doing something they all enjoyed. Finally, they received permission to stay in America permanently. But they missed having a home of their own. They could get along on the money they earned, but it looked as if they would never be able to save enough to buy a house.

Then, quite unexpectedly, they were offered a farm at a price they could just afford. It was in Vermont, in mountain country that reminded them of Austria. There was enough land for them to farm, and they set to work to build themselves a new home.

Everyone settled in very happily and much more quickly than they expected.

There were still long periods when the family had to be away from home on concert tours. It was not an easy time for them. When the United States entered the war against Germany, Rupert and Werner were called up, so the choir lost two voices. Petrol was rationed and few trains were running, so it was difficult to get about, but somehow they always managed.

Once the war was over, the von Trapps began to get distressing letters from Europe. They learned that in their beloved Austria whole towns and villages had been destroyed by bombs and fires. People had no food or medicines, no warm clothes, and little shelter to protect them in the bitter months of winter.

"We must do something," said Captain von Trapp, but he knew that his family made only just enough money to live on. How could they help?

Maria, as always, had an idea. "If the American people learn from us about this terrible suffering, I know they will want to help. They have always been kind and generous to us," she reminded them. "I'm sure they will give money and food and clothing. Wherever we go to sing, we must talk to people and ask for their help."

It seemed a wonderful idea. Maria wrote to Vienna for the addresses of thousands of needy people, and as the von Trapps travelled across the country they talked about the problems of Austria to everyone they met. They held radio and newspaper interviews, distributed leaflets at their concerts, and made appeals in the intervals. Maria asked the audiences to bring whatever they could spare and the family would pack it up and send it off.

The gifts came pouring in. The von Trapps' blue bus was sometimes packed so full with clothes and food and toys that the children could hardly squeeze in.

On the journey between one concert performance and the next, the whole family worked hard sorting the gifts into bags and parcels, wrapping them up, tying the string, addressing the labels and sticking on the stamps. Some of the post offices in the small towns they visited had never seen anything like it, when the von Trapp children came in with pile after pile of packages.

Later they had to reply to the countless thank you letters which came from all the families whom they had helped.

The von Trapps didn't mind the hard work. They felt lucky to be in America – and to be together again, now that Rupert and Werner had come home safe and sound from the war.

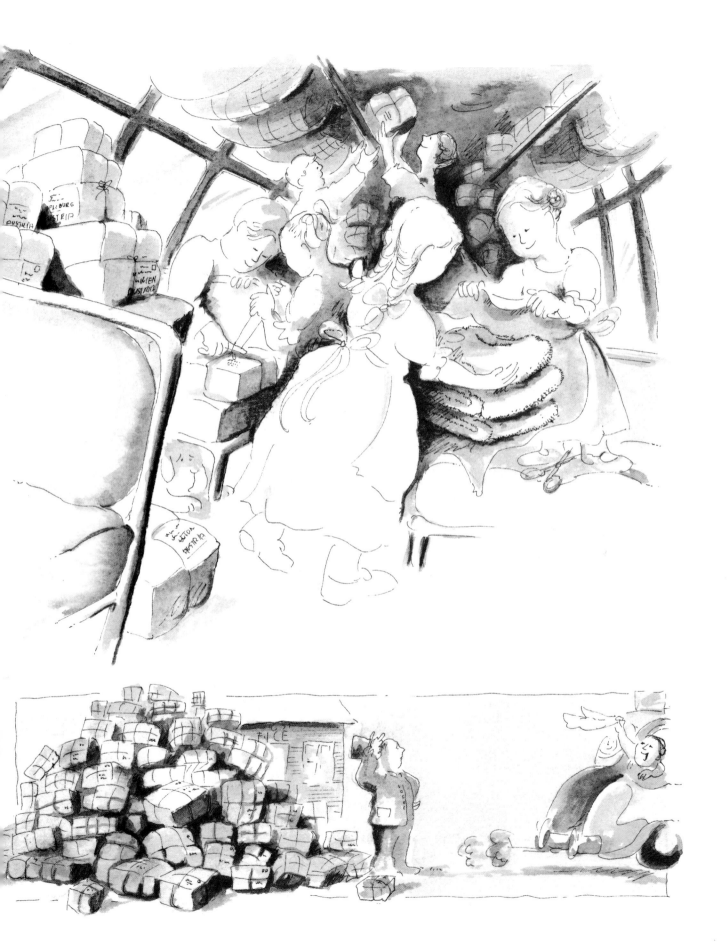

For more than two years,
shipload after shipload of clothes
and food was sent to Austria. It

was a lot of effort, but with every parcel the family knew that not only were they helping to save lives and heal wounds but also to restore the hope without which no one can live happily.

About the von Trapp Family

This is a retelling of a true story and the von Trapps are real people.

When the von Trapps began their travels round America in the big blue bus, they called themselves *The Trapp Family Singers* and dropped the "von" from their name because it was easier for their American friends. Father Wasner, who later became Monsignore Wasner, was the musical director of the choir.

The von Trapp family gave their last public concert in 1955. For twenty years they had entertained people with their music in thirty different countries. After their musical career came to an end, the von Trapps converted the family home in Vermont into a hotel.

Now Captain Georg von Trapp is dead and so are two of his children, Martina and Hedwig.

Maria is still alive and well and the others who were children in this story are living in the United States, in Austria, and, indeed, in many parts of the world, and have children of their own.

The songs which appear on the following pages are a selection of folk tunes from around the world. They are all old traditional songs which have been handed down through many generations and are the kind of songs the von Trapp family loved to sing.

Sarie Marais

South African folk song

My Sa-rie Ma-rais is so far away from me, And I'm long-ing to see her a-gain. She

CHORUS.

lives in a valley by the ri — ver Mooi, Her heart, like mine, is filled with pain. I

long to be in the old Trans-vaal, Back in the land where I was born. I

see my Sa rie sit-ting 'neath the green thorn tree, There 'midst the fields of corn. I

see my darling weeping o so bitterly for me Un-til the day when I'll be free.

Lilli Burlero

English folk song

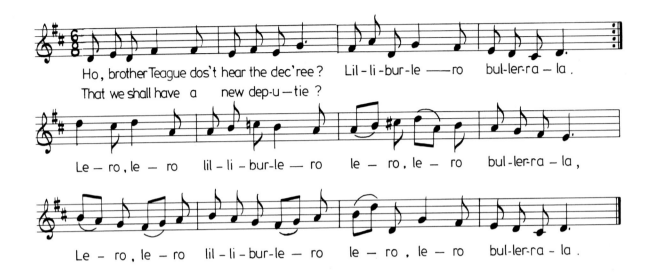

Ho, brother Teague dos't hear the dec'ree? Lil-li-bur-le——ro bul-ler-ra—la.

That we shall have a new dep-u—tie?

Le—ro, le—ro lil-li-bur-le—ro le—ro, le—ro bul-ler-ra—la,

Le—ro, le—ro lil-li-bur-le—ro le—ro, le—ro bul-ler-ra—la.

Waltzing Matilda
Australian folk song

Once a jol-ly swagman camped by a bill-a-bong, Un — der the shade of a

cooli — bah tree; And he sang as he watched and waited till his bil-ly boiled,

CHORUS

"You'll come a-waltzing Ma — til-da with me!" "Waltzing Ma-til-da, waltzing Ma-til-da,

You'll come a-waltz-ing Ma — til — da with me", And he sang as he watched and

waited till his bil-ly boiled,"You'll come a-waltz — ing Ma — til — da with me!"

2. Down came a jumbuck to drink at the billabong,
   Up jumped the swagman and grabbed him with glee;
   And he sang as he shoved that jumbuck in his tucker-bag,
   "You'll come a-waltzing Matilda with me!"

3. Up rode the squatter mounted on his thoroughbred;
   Down came the troopers – one, two and three.
   "Whose the jolly jumbuck you've got in your tucker-bag?
   You'll come a-waltzing Matilda with me."

4. Up jumped the swagman, sprang into the billabong,
   "You'll never catch me alive," said he.
   And his ghost may be heard as you pass by that billabong,
   "Who'll come a-waltzing Matilda with me?"

Yankee Doodle

American folk song

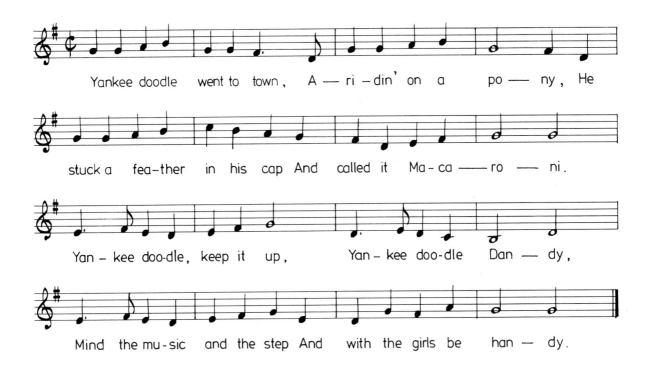

Yankee doodle went to town, A — ri –din' on a po — ny, He

stuck a fea–ther in his cap And called it Ma - ca — ro — ni.

Yan – kee doo-dle, keep it up, Yan – kee doo-dle Dan — dy,

Mind the mu-sic and the step And with the girls be han — dy.

Auld Lang Syne
Traditional Scottish song

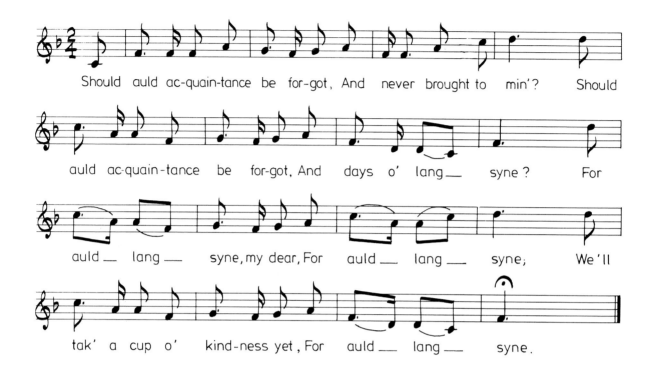

Should auld ac-quain-tance be for-got, And never brought to min'? Should

auld ac-quain-tance be for-got, And days o' lang syne? For

auld lang syne, my dear, For auld lang syne; We'll

tak' a cup o' kind-ness yet, For auld lang syne.

2. We twa hae run about the braes,
And pu'd the gowans fine;
But we've wander'd mony a weary foot,
Sin' auld lang syne.
For auld lang syne, *etc.*

3. And there's a hand, my trusty frien',
And gie's a hand o' thine;
And we'll tak' a right gude willy-waught
For auld lang syne.
For auld lang syne, *etc.*

4. And surely ye'll be your pint stoup,
And surely I'll be mine!
And we'll tak' a cup o' kindness yet,
For auld lang syne.
For auld lang syne, *etc.*

Acknowledgements

For their co-operation and help in the research for this book the author and publisher wish to thank especially Mr. F. C. Schang, the former manager of the "Trapp Family Singers" as well as the staff and management of the following institutes: Oesterreichisches Staatsarchiv, Vienna; Universitaetsbibliothek, Salzburg; Salzburger Nachrichten, Salzburg; Associated Press, New York; New York Public Library for Performing Arts and the Morristown Centennial Library in Vermont.

Rosemarie looking after the pigs   Sleigh ride with winter guests

The Trapp Family house in Vermont, USA which later became a famous hotel and which was burnt down in December 1980